★ *Voices from the Civil War* ★

UNION GENERALS

edited by Tom Head

BLACKBIRCH®
PRESS

THOMSON
★
™
GALE

San Diego • Detroit • New York • San Francisco • Cleveland
New Haven, Conn. • Waterville, Maine • London • Munich

LIBRARY OF CONGRESS CATALOGING-IN-PUBLICATION DATA

Head, Tom.
 Union generals / by Tom Head.
   p. cm. — (Voices from the Civil War)
Summary: Provides excerpts from letters, books, newspaper articles, speeches, and diaries which express various thoughts about the strategies, battles, personalities, and politics of generals during the Civil War.
Includes bibliographical references and index.
 ISBN 1-56711-795-3 (hardback : alk. paper)
 1. Generals—United States—Biography—Juvenile literature. 2. United States. Army—Biography—Juvenile literature. 3. United States—History—Civil War, 1861–1865—Personal narratives—Juvenile literature. [1. Generals. 2. United States—History—Civil War, 1861–1865—Personal narratives. 3. United States—History—Civil War, 1861–1865—Sources.] I. Title. II. Series.

E467.H425 2003
 973.7′3′0922—dc21
                                          2002153710

Printed in United States
10 9 8 7 6 5 4 3 2 1

Contents

★ *Introduction* ★

CHAMPIONS OF THE REPUBLIC

W hen the Civil War broke out in April 1861, military leaders who had dedicated their lives to serving the whole United States suddenly found themselves at war with part of it. Most of the established generation of military leaders on both sides were veterans of the Mexican-American War (1846–1848), in which the United States fought Mexico over control of Texas. Many Union and Confederate generals had graduated from the same military academies. They had fought side-by-side in earlier conflicts, and had become friends. The outbreak of the Civil War forced them to go to war against each other.

During the first months of the war, Union generals believed that the Confederacy was too weak and poorly organized to fight a long war. Many assumed that one or two Union victories would end the rebellion and restore the United States. This belief was shattered at the Battle of Manassas (Bull Run) in July 1861. There, the South won a decisive victory and showed the strength and resolve of the Confederate army.

After the defeat at Manassas, Union military leaders created the massive new Army of the Potomac to protect the Union from invasion. Its first leader was George McClellan, a veteran of the Mexican-American War. McClellan had become well known as an inventor as well as a scholar of military history.

At that time, the general-in-chief of U.S. armed forces was seventy-four-year-old Winfield Scott. Scott was a veteran of the War of 1812. He had served as leader of the U.S. military for twenty years. Although he felt his health was too poor to allow him to lead the Union through the Civil War, he did help set up the Union defense of Washington, D.C. He also outlined the broad strategy that the Union would eventually use to win the war. He retired from military service in November 1861,

Gen. George McClellan was placed in charge of the Army of the Potomac, whose mission was to protect the North from invasion by the Confederacy.

and was replaced by McClellan. Serving as commander of the Army of the Potomac and general-in-chief of Union forces at the same time proved to be impossible, so McClellan stepped down as general-in-chief. He was replaced by Henry Halleck. McClellan continued to serve as commander of the Army of the Potomac.

The first year of the war ended with the Battle of Shiloh, fought in Tennessee in April 1862. Although Union forces were victorious, the twenty-eight thousand battlefield casualties put to rest any Union hopes of a short, low-casualty conflict.

McClellan's policy to win by overwhelming force seemed like a good strategy, but it was a difficult practical goal to achieve. Because of brilliant Confederate tactics that led Union strategists to overestimate the size of Southern armies, McClellan missed several opportunities to crush smaller Confederate armies and potentially end the war. After he failed to follow Robert E. Lee's retreating army after a Union victory at the Battle of Antietam in September 1862, President Abraham Lincoln relieved him of command. Lincoln then placed the Army of the Potomac under the leadership of a reluctant military engineer, General Ambrose Burnside.

Burnside never felt qualified to lead Union forces, but he did the best he could. After a crushing defeat by Robert E. Lee and his Army of Northern Virginia at the Battle of Fredericksburg in December 1862, Burnside accepted full responsibility for the failure and asked to be relieved of command.

His replacement was Joseph "Fightin' Joe" Hooker, a general best known for his

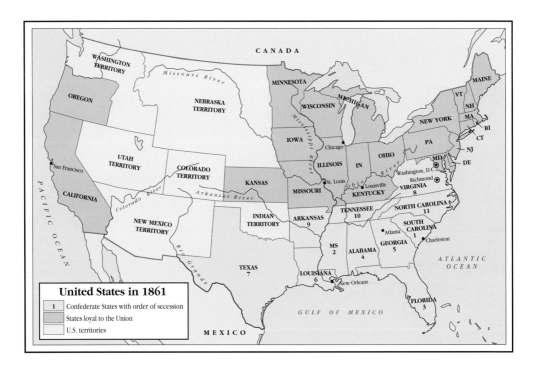

This illustration depicts the Battle of Chancellorsville, Virginia, in May 1863, where the Union Army of the Potomac was routed by rebel forces. Afterward, the leader of the Union forces, Gen. Joseph Hooker, resigned his command.

outrageous belief that the Union should become a military dictatorship. Lincoln warned him that "only those generals who gain successes set up dictators," and put him to work with one primary goal in mind: stamp out Robert E. Lee's deadly Army of Northern Virginia. Hooker launched an assault against Lee's forces at the Battle of Chancellorsville in May 1863. Although his army outnumbered Lee's by almost two-to-one, his attack was a dismal failure. The Army of the Potomac was forced into an embarrassing retreat. Hooker stepped down a month later, and his replacement as leader of the Army of the Potomac was General George Gordon Meade.

When Meade took command of Union forces in June 1863, his track record as a general was not particularly promising. In 1862, he was one of the few generals to be severely wounded three times in the same battle and survive. His leadership at the disastrous Union defeats in Fredericksburg and Chancellorsville was unremarkable. Only a few weeks after taking command of the Army of the Potomac, Meade received word that his men were about to face a major surprise assault from Confederate forces in the little town of Gettysburg, Pennsylvania.

The three-day Battle of Gettysburg was the bloodiest of the war. Fifty-one thousand soldiers became casualties. To Meade's credit, the Union held its ground and forced the weakened Confederate forces into a limping retreat. Meade's luck had turned. Only a day later, on July 4, 1863, Union general Ulysses S. Grant led a force that took control of the Confederate stronghold of Vicksburg, Mississippi.

Meade continued to lead the Army of the Potomac until the end of the war. The role of general-in-chief was still filled by General Henry Halleck. He oversaw the War Department, but did not lead troops on the battlefield. Lincoln felt that a more hands-on form of leadership might benefit the Union cause, so in March 1864, he made General Ulysses S. Grant general-in-chief of Union forces and ordered him to travel with Meade's Army of the Potomac.

By the time Grant took command, he had become known as the most brutal and aggressive Union general of the war. When Grant took up the Union cause, the assertive military aspect of his personality that had shone during the Mexican-American War began to reemerge. His willingness to stare down Confederate leaders and demand surrender on his terms earned him the nickname "Unconditional Surrender" Grant.

The Union strategy during the final year of the war was extremely aggressive, risky, and effective. Grant knew that the Union had more available replacement troops than the Confederacy, so he decided to use the Army of the Potomac to stalk and wear down Lee's Army of Northern Virginia. Meanwhile, other Union generals began to attack civilian resources in an effort to weaken Confederate supply and morale. General William Tecumseh Sherman left a trail of destruction across Georgia during his vicious "March to the Sea." Cavalry leader General Philip Sheridan attacked Confederate farms in Virginia.

The Union strategy proved highly effective. Confederate forces were unable to keep a steady supply of food and equipment. Lee's Army of Northern Virginia was gradually worn down by Grant's Army of the Potomac. On April 9, 1865, Robert E. Lee surrendered, and the Civil War came to an end. The Union generals and their troops had emerged victorious.

On April 9, 1865, Ulysses S. Grant (left) accepted Confederate general Robert E. Lee's (right) surrender at Appomattox Courthouse, Virginia, ending the Civil War.

★ Chronology of the Civil War ★

November 1860	December 1860–March 1861	April 1861

Abraham Lincoln is elected president of the United States.

• Concerned about Lincoln's policy against slavery in the West, the South Carolina legislature unanimously votes to secede from the United States. Alabama, Florida, Georgia, Louisiana, Mississippi, and Texas secede from the Union, and form the Confederate States of America.

• Mississippi senator Jefferson Davis becomes president of the Confederacy.

• Arkansas, North Carolina, Tennessee, and Virginia later join the rebellion.

Confederate troops fire on Union-occupied Fort Sumter in South Carolina and force a surrender. This hostile act begins the Civil War.

September 1862–January 1863

• Lee's Army of Northern Virginia and George McClellan's Army of the Potomac fight the war's bloodiest one-day battle at Antietam, Maryland. Though the battle is a draw, Lee's forces retreat to Virginia.

• Abraham Lincoln issues the Emancipation Proclamation that declares all slaves in Confederate states to be forever free. Three months later it takes effect.

September 1864

Atlanta, Georgia, surrenders to Union general William T. Sherman, who orders Atlanta evacuated and then burned. Over the coming months, he begins his March to the Sea to Savannah. His troops destroy an estimated $100 million worth of civilian property in an attempt to cut rebel supply lines and reduce morale.

Jefferson Davis, president of the Confederate States of America

July 1861

Confederate troops defeat Union forces at the First Battle of Manassas (First Bull Run) in Fairfax County, Virginia, the first large-scale battle of the war.

April 1862

- Confederate troops are defeated at the Battle of Shiloh in Tennessee. An estimated 23,750 soldiers are killed, wounded, or missing, more than in all previous American wars combined.

- Slavery is officially abolished in the District of Columbia; the only Union slave states left are Delaware, Kentucky, Maryland, and Missouri.

June 1862

General Robert E. Lee assumes command of the Conferate Army of Northern Virginia.

Robert E. Lee

August 1862

Confederate troops defeat Union forces at the Second Battle of Manassas (Second Bull Run) in Prince William County, Virginia.

July 1863

Union forces stop the South's invasion of the North at Gettysburg, Pennsylvania. Lasting three days, it is the bloodiest battle of the war.

November 1863

President Abraham Lincoln delivers the Gettysburg Address in honor of those who died at the war's bloodiest battle at Gettysburg.

April 1865

- Confederate general Robert E. Lee surrenders to Union general Ulysses S. Grant. This ends the Civil War on April 9.

- Five days later, President Lincoln is assassinated by actor John Wilkes Booth.

December 1865

The Thirteenth Amendment becomes law and abolishes slavery in the United States.

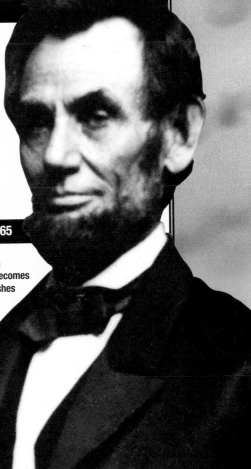

Abraham Lincoln, president of the United States of America

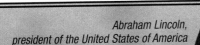

★ Robert Anderson ★

THE SURRENDER OF FORT SUMTER

When the Confederate States of America came into existence in February 1861, it began to claim U.S. military forts and equipment in Southern states. Robert Anderson, a proslavery Southerner who nonetheless remained loyal to the Union, was asked to prevent the Confederacy from taking control of military bases in Charleston Harbor, South Carolina. For five weeks, he and his troops made camp in Fort Moultrie. He then moved to Fort Sumter, which was located on higher ground and was therefore harder to claim by force. When Confederate general P.G.T. Beauregard called for Anderson's surrender, he refused. Beauregard ordered the Confederate troops who occupied Fort Moultrie to fire on Fort Sumter. Thirty-four hours later, Anderson and his exhausted troops surrendered their heavily damaged fort. In this excerpt from his official report, Anderson explains his decision to surrender.

- **Robert Anderson, Report on the Battle of Fort Sumter (April 15, 1861), in *The War of the Rebellion*, series I, 53 volumes. Washington: Government Printing Office, 1880–1901.**

April 18:] Having defended Fort Sumter for thirty-four hours, until the quarters were entirely burned, the main gates destroyed by fire, the gorge walls seriously injured, the magazine surrounded by flames, and its door closed from the effects of heat, four barrels and three cartridges of powder only being available, and no provisions remaining but pork, I accepted terms of evacuation offered by General Beauregard . . . and marched out of the fort Sunday afternoon . . . with colors flying and drums beating, bringing away company and private property, and saluting my flag with fifty guns. . . .

Maj. Robert Anderson was in charge of Fort Sumter in April 1861.

This print portrays Union soldiers firing cannons in defense of Fort Sumter against attack by Confederate troops in April 1861. The battle and subsequent surrender of the fort marked the start of the Civil War.

[April 19:] Fort Sumter is left in ruins from the effect of the shell and shot from [Beauregard's] batteries, and officers of his army reported that our firing had destroyed most of the buildings inside Fort Moultrie. God was pleased to guard my little force from the shell and shot which were thrown into and against my work, and to Him are our thanks due that I am enabled to report that no one was seriously injured by their fire. I regret that I have to add that, in consequence of some unaccountable misfortune, one man was killed, two seriously and three slightly wounded whilst saluting our flag as it was lowered.

GLOSSARY

- **gorge:** entrance to the fort
- **magazine:** ammunition storehouse
- **in consequence of:** because of

★ *Winfield Scott* ★
PREPARE FOR A LONG WAR

Gen. Winfield Scott was the most experienced general in the Union.

Nicknamed "Old Fuss and Feathers" by his soldiers, Winfield Scott had served for twenty years as leader of the U.S. armed forces when the Civil War broke out. It quickly became clear to him that he was, at age seventy-four, not healthy enough to lead the army himself. As the most experienced and skilled general in the country, however, he felt morally bound to advise the younger generals on the strategy he felt would best serve the Union. His broad strategy—to secure New Orleans and block off the Mississippi River while gradually building a large army—was adopted by later Union generals. In this letter to George McClellan, who later took over command of Union forces, Scott recommends patience and gradual preparation for a long war.

- **Winfield Scott, Letter to George B. McClellan (May 3, 1861), in *The War of the Rebellion*, series I, 53 volumes. Washington: Government Printing Office, 1880–1901.**

A word now as to the greatest obstacle in the way of this plan—the great danger now pressing upon us—the impatience of our patriotic and loyal Union friends. They will urge instant and vigorous action, regardless, I fear, of consequences—that is, unwilling to wait for the slow instruction of (say) twelve or fifteen camps, for the rise of rivers, and the return of frosts to kill the virus of malignant fevers below Memphis. I fear this; but impress right views, on every proper occasion, upon the brave men who are hastening to the support of their Government. Lose no time, while necessary preparations for the great expedition are in progress, in organizing, drilling, and disciplining your three-months' men, many of whom, it is hoped, will be ultimately found enrolled under the call for three-years' volunteers. Should an urgent and immediate occasion arise meantime for their services, they will be the more effective.

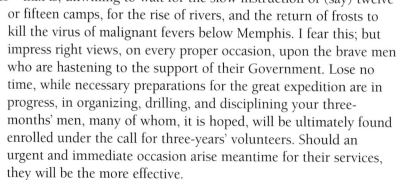

GLOSSARY
- **malignant:** life-threatening
- **impress:** force
- **three-months' men:** Union volunteers who signed up to fight for three months

★ George McClellan ★

TO WIN BY OVERWHELMING FORCE

At the beginning of the Civil War, George McClellan was one of the most educated and promising officers in the Union. McClellan was the obvious choice to replace Winfield Scott as commander of Union forces. Even before McClellan took command, President Abraham Lincoln had already sought his advice on war strategy, which he provided in this August 1861 report. McClellan argues that the Union can win the Civil War by gathering up massive forces to overwhelm Southern armies. This will encourage an early surrender and lower casualties on both sides. The next year, McClellan called upon the government to supply more and more troops if he was to win by "overwhelming physical force." When McClellan waited for reinforcements, rather than following up on a possible opportunity to crush Southern armies and end the war, Lincoln removed him from command.

- **George B. McClellan, *Report upon the Organization of the Army of the Potomac, and Its Campaigns in Virginia and Maryland, from July 26, 1861 to November 7, 1862*. Chicago: Times, 1864.**

The object of the present war differs from those in which nations are engaged, mainly in this: that the purpose of ordinary war is to conquer a peace, and make a treaty on advantageous terms; in this contest it has become necessary to crush a population sufficiently numerous, intelligent and war-like to constitute a nation. We have not only to defeat their armed and organized forces in the field, but to display such an overwhelming strength as will convince all our antagonists, especially those of the governing, aristocratic class, of the utter impossibility of resistance. Our late reverses make this course imperative. Had we been successful in the recent battle [at Manassas, Virginia], it is possible that we might have been spared the labor and expenses of a great effort.

Now we have no alternative. Their success will enable the political leaders of the rebels to convince the mass of their people that we are inferior to them in force and courage, and to command all their resources. The contest began with a class, now it is with a people—our military success can alone restore the former issue.

By thoroughly defeating their armies, taking their strong places, and pursuing a rigidly protective policy as to private property and unarmed persons, and a lenient course as to private soldiers, we may well hope for a permanent restoration of a peaceful Union. But, in the first instance, the authority of the government must be supported by overwhelming physical force.

GLOSSARY
- **antagonists:** enemies
- **aristocratic:** high born
- **late reverses:** recent setbacks
- **imperative:** crucial
- **rebels:** Confederates
- **lenient:** not strict

★ *Benjamin Franklin Butler* ★
THE FATE OF CAPTURED SLAVES

In early 1861, General Benjamin Butler captured Confederate slave laborers and put them to work for the Union. This was against Union policy, which forbade Union troops from "harboring fugitive slaves." In this letter to the secretary of war, Butler argues against the policy. Congress later passed the First Confiscation Act, which states that slaves employed by the Confederate army would not be considered "fugitives."

● **Benjamin Butler, Report on Contrabands of War, 1861.**

GLOSSARY

● **in a great measure:** largely
● **thither:** there
● **marauding:** raiding
● **rebels:** Confederates
● **batteries:** artillery placements
● **intrenchments:** trenches
● **zealously:** devotedly
● **subsistence:** room and board
● **rendered:** made
● **obliged:** forced
● **liable:** legally appropriate
● **relicts:** remnants
● **relinquished:** surrendered, given up
● **compelled:** forced
● **manumitted:** freed from slavery
● **therein:** there
● **steadfastly:** firmly
● **discretion:** judgment

In the village of Hampton [Virginia] there were a large number of negroes, composed in a great measure of women and children of the men who had fled thither within my lines for protection, who had escaped from marauding parties of rebels, who had been gathering up able-bodied blacks to aid them in constructing their batteries. . . . I had employed the men in Hampton in throwing up intrenchments, and they were working zealously and efficiently at that duty, saving our soldiers from that labor under the gleam of the mid-day sun. The women were earning substantially their own subsistence in washing, marketing, and taking care of the clothes of the soldiers, and rations were being served out to the men who worked for the support of the children. But by the evacuation of Hampton, rendered necessary by the withdrawal of troops, leaving me scarcely five thousand men outside the fort including the force at Newport News, all these black people were obliged to break up their homes at Hampton, fleeing across the creek within my lines for protection and support.

Are these men, women, and children slaves? Are they free? Is their condition that of men, women, and children, or of property, or is it a mixed relation? What their status was under the constitution and laws, we all know. What has been the effect of a rebellion and a state of war upon that status? When I adopted the theory of treating the able-bodied negro fit to work in the trenches as property liable to be used in aid of rebellion, and so contraband of war, that condition of things was in so far met, as I then and still believe, on a legal and constitutional basis. But now a new series of questions arise. Passing by women, the children, certainly, cannot be treated on that basis; if property, they must be considered the incumbrance rather than the

Escaped slaves like these were deemed contraband of war by Union general Benjamin Franklin Butler.

auxiliary of an army, and, of course, in no possible legal relation could be treated as contraband. Are they property? If they were so, they have been left by their masters and owners, deserted, thrown away, abandoned, like the wrecked vessel upon the ocean. Their former possessors and owners have causelessly, traitorously, rebelliously, and, to carry out the figure, practically abandoned them to be swallowed up by the winter storm of starvation. . . . Have they not become, thereupon, men, women, and children? No longer under ownership of any kind, the fearful relicts of fugitive masters, have they not by their master's acts, and the state of war, assumed the condition, which we hold to be the normal one, of those made in God's image? Is not every constitutional, legal, and normal requirement, as well to the runaway master as their relinquished slaves, thus answered? I confess that my own mind is compelled by this reasoning to look upon them as men and women. If not free born, yet free, manumitted, sent forth from the hand that held them, never to be reclaimed.

Of course, if this reasoning, thus imperfectly set forth, is correct, my duty as a humane man is very plain. I should take the same care of these men, women, and children, houseless, homeless, and unprovided for, as I would of the same number of men, women, and children, who, for their attachment to the Union, had been driven or allowed to flee from the Confederate States. I should have no doubt on this question had I not seen it stated that an order had been issued by General McDowell in his department substantially forbidding all fugitive slaves from coming within his lines, or being harbored there. Is that order to be enforced in all military departments? If so, who are to be considered fugitive whose master runs away and leaves him? Is it forbidden to the troops to aid or harbor within their lines the negro children who are found therein, or is the soldier, when his march has destroyed their means of subsistence, to allow them to starve because he has driven off the rebel masters? Now, shall the commander of a regiment or battalion sit in judgment upon the question, whether any given black man has fled from his master, or his master fled from him? Indeed, how are the free born to be distinguished? Is one any more or less a fugitive slave because he has labored upon the rebel intrenchments? . . .

I have very decided opinions upon the subject of this order. It does not become me to criticise it, and I write in no spirit of criticism, but simply to explain the full difficulties that surround the enforcing it if the enforcement of that order becomes the policy of the government. I, as a soldier, shall be bound to enforce it steadfastly, if not cheerfully. But if left to my own discretion, as you may have gathered from my reasoning, I should take a widely different course from that which it indicates.

★ *Ambrose Burnside* ★

THE DEFEAT AT FREDERICKSBURG

Ambrose Burnside

When Ambrose Burnside was offered command of the Army of the Potomac (the Union's largest army) in October 1862, he accepted the position reluctantly. President Abraham Lincoln, however, had complete confidence in him as a general. In December 1862, Burnside planned an attack on Robert E. Lee's forces near Fredericksburg, Virginia. The Confederate army was well protected in fortifications, and the Union attack failed. Having suffered more than thirteen thousand casualties, Burnside's men were forced to retreat. Burnside wrote this letter to the War Department, apologizing for the heavy losses and taking full responsibility for the failure.

- **Ambrose Burnside, Letter to Army Headquarters (December 17, 1862), in *The War of the Rebellion*, series I, 53 volumes. Washington: Government Printing Office, 1880–1901.**

How near we came to accomplishing our object future reports will show. . . . As it was, we came very near success. Failing in accomplishing the main object, we remained in order of battle two days—long enough to decide that the enemy would not come out of his strongholds and fight us with his infantry. After which we recrossed to this side of the river unmolested, and without the loss of men or property. As the day broke, our long lines of troops were seen marching to their different positions as if going on parade; not the least demoralization or disorganization existed. To the brave officers and soldiers who accomplished the feat of this recrossing in the face of the enemy I owe everything. For the failure in the attack I am responsible, as the extreme gallantry, courage, and endurance shown by them was never excelled, and would have carried the points, had it been possible.

To the families and friends of the dead I can only offer my heartfelt sympathy, but for the wounded I can offer my earnest prayers for their comfort and final recovery. . . .

I will visit you very soon and give you more definite information, and finally will send you my detailed report, in which a special acknowledgment will be made of the services of the different grand divisions, corps, and my general and personal staff departments of the Army of the Potomac, to whom I am much indebted for their hearty support and co-operation.

GLOSSARY

- **object:** goal, objective
- **in order of battle:** awaiting a fight
- **strongholds:** fortifications
- **demoralization:** poor fighting spirit
- **points:** forts
- **earnest:** sincere

★ *Joseph Hooker* ★

THE DEFEAT AT CHANCELLORSVILLE

In January 1863, President Abraham Lincoln placed Joseph Hooker in command of the Army of the Potomac. Hooker immediately began to reorganize Union forces in preparation for an assault on Robert E. Lee's forces in Virginia. Two months later, the Army of the Potomac attacked Lee's forces near the city of Chancellorsville, Virginia. With skill, bravery, and luck, Lee's army of fifty-seven thousand effectively defeated Hooker's army of one hundred thousand. Of Hooker's army, fourteen thousand troops were injured or killed, and the rest retreated. Hooker, who had probably suffered a severe head injury during the battle, considered it a victory. In this strange letter to his troops, Hooker applauds them for their "achievements." He stepped down as head of the Army of the Potomac in June 1863.

- **Joseph Hooker, "General Orders, No. 49," in *The War of the Rebellion*, series I, 53 volumes. Washington: Government Printing Office, 1880–1901.**

The major-general commanding tenders to this army his congratulations on its achievements of the last seven days. If it has not accomplished all that was expected, the reasons are well known to the army. It is sufficient to say they were of a character not to be foreseen or prevented by human sagacity or resource.

In withdrawing from the south bank of the Rappahannock [River] before delivering a general battle to our adversaries, the army has given renewed evidence of its confidence in itself and its fidelity to the principles it represents. In fighting at a disadvantage, we would have been recreant to our trust, to ourselves, our cause, and our country.

Profoundly loyal, and conscious of its strength, the Army of the Potomac will give or decline battle whenever its interest or honor may demand. It will also be the guardian of its own history and its own fame.

By our celerity and secrecy of movement, our advance and passage of the rivers were undisputed, and on our withdrawal not a rebel ventured to follow.

The events of the last week may swell with pride the heart of every officer and soldier of this army. We have added new luster to its former renown. We have made long marches, crossed rivers, surprised the enemy in his intrenchments, and whenever we have fought have inflicted heavier blows than we have received. . . .

We have no other regret than that caused by the loss of our brave companions, and in this we are consoled by the conviction that they have fallen in the holiest cause ever submitted to the arbitrament of battle.

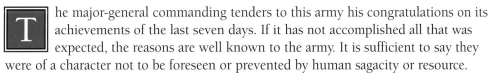

GLOSSARY

- **tenders:** gives
- **sagacity:** wisdom
- **adversaries:** enemies
- **fidelity:** loyalty
- **recreant:** cowardly
- **celerity:** swiftness
- **undisputed:** unopposed
- **rebel:** Confederate
- **conviction:** firm belief
- **arbitrament:** judgment

★ *Horace Porter* ★

GRANT AT THE DINNER TABLE

Horace Porter graduated from a military academy in 1860, only to see the Civil War break out a year later. Porter quickly established himself as a brilliant and courageous military leader. His gallant efforts at the Battle of Chickamauga in 1863 earned him a Congressional Medal of Honor. He was made a full general in March 1865. Although Porter's military skills were impressive, he is better known for his work as an aide to Ulysses S. Grant. In Grant's camp, each high-ranking officer served as caterer for a month and was expected to keep the cooks instructed on what other officers liked to eat. In this excerpt from his 1897 war memoirs, Porter recalls his month as caterer and an assignment that proved a challenge to his great military mind: keeping Grant fed.

• **Horace Porter, *Campaigning with Grant*. New York: Century, 1897.**

T he general, while he never complained, was still the most difficult person to cater for in the whole army. About the only meat he enjoyed was beef, and this he could not eat unless it was so thoroughly well done that no appearance of blood could be seen. If blood appeared in any meat which came on the table, the sight of it seemed entirely to destroy his appetite. (This was the man whose enemies delighted in calling him a butcher.) He enjoyed oysters and fruit, but these could not be procured on an active campaign. He never ate mutton when he could obtain anything else, and fowl and game he abhorred. As he used to express it: "I never could eat anything that goes on two legs."

He ate less than any man in the army; sometimes the amount of food taken did not seem enough to keep a bird alive, and his meals were frugal enough to satisfy the tastes of the most avowed anchorite. It so happened that no one in the mess had any inclination to drink wine or spirits at meals, and none was carried among the mess's supplies. The only beverage ever used at table besides tea and coffee was water, although on the march it was often taken from places which rendered it not the most palatable or healthful of drinks. If a staff-officer wanted anything stronger he would carry some commissary whisky in a canteen. Upon a few occasions, after a hard day's ride in stormy weather, the general joined the officers of the staff in taking a whisky toddy in the evening. He never offered liquor of any kind to visitors at headquarters. His hospitality consisted in inviting them to meals and to smoke cigars.

🖋 GLOSSARY

- **abhorred:** detested
- **frugal:** scanty
- **anchorite:** monk
- **mess:** army kitchen
- **inclination:** desire
- **spirits:** liquor
- **palatable:** pleasant-tasting
- **commissary:** military food store
- **toddy:** hot water mixed with liquor, sugar, and spices

★ George Meade ★

MEADE CONGRATULATES HIS ARMY

The Battle of Gettysburg was a major turning point in the Civil War. For months, Robert E. Lee had embarrassed the Union army by defeating it in a series of costly battles. At Gettysburg, Pennsylvania, the tide turned, and Lee was forced to retreat after three days of bloody fighting that claimed fifty-one thousand Union and Confederate casualties. George Meade was one of the Union leaders at Gettysburg. Meade had served with distinction throughout the war, but this was a rare opportunity for him to take credit for a major success. His luck up to the first week of July 1863, had been anything but promising. In this letter to his troops, he congratulates them on their history-making performance. Meade did not get to bask in the glory of victory for long, though. President Abraham Lincoln objected to his use of the phrase "our soil" in this letter (which implied that only the Northern states were part of the Union) and, within days, Meade was severely criticized for not following Lee's army as it retreated to Virginia. Meade offered his resignation, but Lincoln refused to accept it. Meade remained commander of the Army of the Potomac until it was disbanded at the end of the war.

George Meade

• **George Gordon Meade, "General Orders, No. 68," in *The War of the Rebellion*, series I, 53 volumes. Washington: Government Printing Office, 1880–1901.**

T he commanding general, in behalf of the country, thanks the Army of the Potomac for the glorious result of the recent operations.

An enemy, superior in numbers, and flushed with the pride of a successful invasion, attempted to overcome and destroy this army. Utterly baffled and defeated, he has now withdrawn from the contest. The privations and fatigue the army has endured, and the heroic courage and gallantry it has displayed, will be matters of history, to be ever remembered.

Our task is not yet accomplished, and the commanding general looks to the army for greater efforts to drive from our soil every vestige of the presence of the invader.

It is right and proper that we should, on all suitable occasions, return our grateful thanks to the Almighty Disposer of events, that in the goodness of his providence He has thought fit to give victory to the cause of the just.

> **GLOSSARY**
> - **baffled:** confused
> - **privations:** losses; sacrifices
> - **vestige:** remnant
> - **Almighty Disposer of events:** God
> - **providence:** care

★ *John Buford* ★
EVENLY MATCHED AT MIDDLEBURG

In June 1863, General Robert E. Lee invaded Pennsylvania with his Army of Northern Virginia. To protect Lee's troops from counterattack, other Confederate forces began to attack Union troops in nearby areas of Virginia and Pennsylvania. On June 16, at the Battle of Middleburg, Virginia, Confederate forces attacked General J. Irvin Gregg's vastly outnumbered 1st Rhode Island Infantry. Union cavalry units, led by John Buford, counterattacked but were driven off by bad terrain. In this excerpt from his report of the Battle of Middleburg, General John Buford explains the events of that day. Like many small Civil War battles, it had no clear winner—the battle simply came to an end, and both Union and Confederate forces proceeded as they had before it began.

- **John Buford, Report on the Battle of Middleburg (June 24, 1863), in *The War of the Rebellion*, series I, 53 volumes. Washington: Government Printing Office, 1880–1901.**

The night was extremely dark. Nearly the whole of the division was on duty, very much divided, and without rations or forage. To concentrate and draw supplies which had arrived during the night, and to move at so short a notice, proved to be impracticable. The command, however, got off shortly after daylight, without supplies, and reached Middleburg in season for the day's operations. The Reserve Brigade . . . joined me at Middleburg.

From Middleburg I started to turn the enemy's left flank. On reaching Goose Creek, I took the command up the right bank of the creek, over a most difficult country, and came up to the enemy on his extreme left, in a position where I could not turn him. I then marched back to the ford, drove the enemy's pickets off, crossed, and started up the creek, intending to recross at Millville. The enemy threw a considerable force (three regiments) in my front to dispute my advance. He was driven steadily before us for some time. . . . I took Colonel Gamble's and Colonel Devin's brigades, and pushed for Upperville. My advance was

Gen. John Buford led the Union forces at the Battle of Middleburg.

An eyewitness's sketch depicts the battle of Upperville, Virginia, where Gen. John Buford sought to aid Gen. J. Irvin Gregg's besieged Union troops in June 1863.

disputed pretty warmly by the enemy, but he made no stand save with his skirmishers. These were severely punished.

When within a mile of Upperville, I saw a large force in front of General Gregg, who appeared to be outnumbered. I resolved to go to his aid. The column struck a brisk trot, but ran afoul of so many obstructions in the shape of ditches and stone fences, that it did not make fast progress, and got out of shape. While in this position, I discovered a train of wagons and a few troops to my right marching at a trot, apparently making for Ashby's Gap. I turned the head of my column toward them, and very soon became engaged with a superior force. The enemy brought four 12-pounder guns into position, and made some excellent practice on the head of my regiments as they came up. The gunners were driven from the guns, which would have fallen into our hands but for two impassable stone fences. The enemy then came up in magnificent style from the direction of Snickersville, and for a time threatened me with overwhelming numbers. He was compelled, however, to retire before the terrific carbine fire which the brave Eighth Illinois and Third Indiana poured into him. As he withdrew, my rear troops came up, formed, and pressed him back to the mountains. He was driven over the mountains into the valley.

I am happy to say that my loss is much smaller than I had reason to suppose. . . . It is small in comparison with that of the enemy.

Toward night I came back, and encamped on the ground which had been so hotly contested. The enemy's dead were buried and his wounded provided for.

GLOSSARY

- **forage:** nearby sources of food
- **turn:** force intro retreat
- **pickets:** soldiers placed in front of a main fighting force
- **skirmishers:** pickets
- **resolved:** decided
- **column:** cavalry formation
- **12-pounder guns:** cannons
- **carbine:** type of rifle given to cavalry men

★ Joshua Lawrence Chamberlain ★
BRAVERY AT LITTLE ROUND TOP

When Professor Joshua Lawrence Chamberlain asked for a leave of absence from Bowdoin College, he lied to the school's administrators. He told them that he planned to study languages in Europe. After gaining their approval, he immediately joined the Thirtieth Maine Infantry and began to work his way up the Union ranks. Chamberlain is best known for his courageous defense of Little Round Top, a strategically important hill in the Battle of Gettysburg. His actions on that day in July 1863 earned him a Congressional Medal of Honor and a place in history as one of the most memorable figures of the battle. In this excerpt from his July 6 report on the battle, Chamberlain describes how his forces had kept Little Round Top from falling into Confederate hands four days earlier.

- **Joshua L. Chamberlain, Report on the Gettysburg Campaign, in *The War of the Rebellion*, series I, 53 volumes. Washington: Government Printing Office, 1880–1901.**

The enemy seemed to have gathered all their energies for their final assault. We had gotten our thin line into as good a shape as possible, when a strong force emerged from the scrub wood in the valley, as well as I could judge, in two lines in échelon by the right, and, opening a heavy fire, the first line came on as if they meant to sweep everything before them. We opened on them as well as we could with our scanty ammunition snatched from the field.

It did not seem possible to withstand another shock like this now coming on. Our loss had been severe [during previous Confederate attempts to take the hill]. One-half of my left wing had fallen, and a third of my regiment lay just behind us, dead or badly wounded. At this moment my anxiety was increased by a great roar of musketry in my rear, on the farther or northerly slope of Little Round Top, apparently on the flank of the regular brigade. . . . I feared that the enemy might have nearly surrounded the Little Round Top, and only a desperate chance was left for us. My ammunition was soon exhausted. My men were firing their last shot and getting ready to "club" [with] their muskets.

It was imperative to strike before we were struck by this overwhelming force in a hand-to-hand fight, which we could not probably have withstood or survived. At that crisis, I ordered

Joshua L. Chamberlain was a Union hero of the Battle of Gettysburg for his courageous defense of Little Round Top.

This engraving shows the intensity of the fighting at Little Round Top, a key battle in the Union victory at Gettysburg in July 1863.

the bayonet. The word was enough. It ran like fire along the line, from man to man, and rose into a shout, with which they sprang forward upon the enemy, now not 30 yards away. The effect was surprising; many of the enemy's first line threw down their arms and surrendered. An officer fired his pistol at my head with one hand, while he handed me his sword with the other. Holding fast by our right, and swinging forward our left, we made an extended "right wheel," before which the enemy's second line broke and fell back, fighting from tree to tree, many being captured, until we had swept the valley and cleared the front of nearly our entire brigade.

Meantime Captain Morrill with his skirmishers (sent out from my left flank), with some dozen or fifteen of the U.S. Sharpshooters who had put themselves under his direction, fell upon the enemy as they were breaking, and by his demonstrations, as well as his well-directed fire, added much to the effect of the charge.

Having thus cleared the valley and driven the enemy up the western slope of the Great Round Top [a larger hill nearby], not wishing to press so far out as to hazard the ground I was to hold by leaving it exposed to a sudden rush of the enemy, I succeeded (although with some effort to stop my men, who declared they were "on the road to Richmond [Confederate capital]") in getting the regiment into good order and resuming our original position.

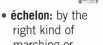

GLOSSARY

- **échelon:** by the right kind of marching or military formation
- **imperative:** necessary
- **ordered the bayonet:** ordered the men to fix their bayonets—long knives—to their rifles and charge
- **skirmishers:** soldiers placed in front of a main fighting force
- **demonstrations:** show of force
- **hazard:** endanger

★ *Ulysses S. Grant* ★
WEARING OUT THE ENEMY

Ulysses S. Grant

On July 4, 1863, troops led by Ulysses S. Grant took control of Vicksburg, Mississippi. Control of the city finally gave the Union command of the Mississippi River. This act effectively cut off the largest and most reliable Confederate supply line and helped bring about a Union victory. It was because of this success, among others, that President Abraham Lincoln placed Grant in command of the entire Union army in March 1864. Almost immediately, Grant and the Army of the Potomac began a long series of battles with Robert E. Lee's Army of Northern Virginia. The battles did not always end as Union victories, but they did inflict high casualties on Lee's forces. Since the South did not have the manpower to replace these losses, Grant's strategy was to wear down Lee's army and force it to surrender. After a day of hard fighting in May 1864, Grant stopped to write this letter to his wife, Julia.

• **Ulysses S. Grant, Letter to His Wife, May 13, 1864.**

Dear Julia, The ninth day of battle is just closing with victory so far on our side. But the enemy are fighting with great desperation entrenching themselves in every position they take up. We have lost many thousand men killed and wounded and the enemy have no doubt lost more. We have taken about eight thousand prisoners and lost likely three thousand. Among our wounded the great majority are but slightly hurt but most of them will be unfit for service in this battle. I have reinforcements now coming up which will greatly encourage our men and discourage the enemy correspondingly.

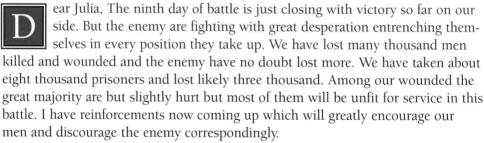

I am very well and full of hope. I see from the papers the country is also hopeful.

Remember me to your father and Aunt Fanny. Kisses for yourself and the children. The world has never seen so bloody or so protracted a battle as the one being fought and I hope never will again. The enemy were really whipped yesterday but their situation is desperate beyond anything heretofore known. To [lose] this battle they [lose] their cause. As bad as it is they have fought for it with a gallantry worthy of a better.

Ulys.

GLOSSARY
• **entrenching themselves:** digging protective trenches
• **protracted:** long
• **heretofore:** until now

★ David G. Farragut ★
DAMN THE TORPEDOES!

David Farragut's career in the U.S. Navy dated from the War of 1812. By the time the Civil War broke out, he was considered the greatest living U.S. naval commander. At the Battle of Mobile Bay, Alabama, on August 5, 1864, Farragut commanded a Union fleet that mounted an assault on the Confederate naval stronghold of Fort Morgan. The fort was guarded by strong cannons, a fleet of ships, and a number of unexploded mines called torpedoes. When a ship in Farragut's fleet was destroyed by a torpedo, other Union ships began to hold off on their advance into the bay. A sailor on Farragut's ship, the Hartford, warned him: "Torpedoes ahead!" Farragut answered, "Damn the torpedoes! Full speed ahead!" Inspired by Farragut's bravery, other Union commanders followed him through the water minefield and took control of Fort Morgan. In this excerpt from his report, Farragut explains his decision to advance.

- **David G. Farragut, Report on the Battle of Mobile Bay (No. 303), Official Records of the Union and Confederate Navies in *The War of the Rebellion*, series I, 53 volumes. Washington: Government Printing Office, 1906.**

I t was soon apparent that there was some difficulty ahead. The *Brooklyn* for some cause which I did not then clearly understand, . . . arrested the advance of the whole fleet, while at the same time the guns of the fort were playing with great effect upon that vessel and the *Hartford*. A moment after I saw the *Tecumseh*, struck by a torpedo, disappear almost instantaneously beneath the waves, carrying with her her gallant commander and nearly all her crew. I determined at once, as I had originally intended, to take the lead, and after ordering the *Metacomet* to send a boat to save, if possible, any of the perishing crew, I dashed ahead with the *Hartford*, and the ships followed on, their officers believing that they were going to a noble death with their commander in chief.

I steamed through between the buoys where the torpedoes were supposed to have been sunk. These buoys had been previously examined by my flag-lieutenant, J. Crittenden Watson, in several nightly reconnaissances. Though he had not been able to discover the sunken torpedoes, yet we had been assured by refugees, deserters, and others of their existence, but believing that from their having been some time in the water, they were probably innocuous, I determined to take the chance of their explosion.

From the moment I turned to the northwestward to clear the Middle Ground we were enabled to keep such a broadside fire upon the batteries at Fort Morgan that their guns did us comparatively little injury.

> **GLOSSARY**
> - **arrested:** stopped
> - **playing:** firing
> - **buoys:** floating beacons used to mark the location of underwater objects
> - **innocuous:** harmless

★ William Tecumseh Sherman ★
WAR IS CRUEL

Regarded by military historians as one of the most gifted strategists of the war, William Tecumseh Sherman worked at a military academy in Louisiana when the Civil War broke out. He came out of retirement to serve the U.S. Army and by 1864, was a full general in command of all Union forces west of the Mississippi River. In September 1864, Sherman's troops took control of Atlanta, Georgia, after a long and bloody battle. Rather than leave troops there to defend the city from a Confederate counterattack, or leave the city's resources intact for future Confederate use, Sherman devised a new strategy: burn the city and move on. In an effort to reduce civilian casualties, Sherman ordered the city evacuated. When leaders of the city wrote to him to beg for mercy, the following letter served as his response. After leaving Atlanta, Sherman led his sixty thousand troops on a rampage through Georgia in his "March to the Sea;" although his strategy unquestionably contributed to the Union's victory, it destroyed Georgia's economy and complicated postwar rebuilding efforts.

Gen. William T. Sherman

• **Letter to James M. Calhoun, E.E. Rawson, and S.C. Wells, in William T. Sherman, *Memoirs of Gen. W.T. Sherman*, 1875.**

 entlemen: I have your letter of the 11th, in the nature of a petition to revoke my orders removing all the inhabitants from Atlanta. I have read it carefully, and give full credit to your statements of the distress that will be occasioned, and yet shall not revoke my orders, because they were not designed to meet the humanities of the case, but to prepare for the future struggles in which millions of good people outside of Atlanta have a deep interest. . . .

You cannot qualify war in harsher terms than I will. War is cruelty, and you cannot refine it; and those who brought war into our country deserve all the curses and maledictions a people can pour out. I know I had no hand in making this war, and I know I will make more sacrifices to-day than any

This photo of Atlanta, Georgia, in September 1864 shows the complete devastation done to it by Gen. William Sherman's "March to the Sea."

of you to secure peace. But you cannot have peace and a division of our country. . . . The United States does and must assert its authority, wherever it once had power; for, if it relaxes one bit to pressure, it is gone, and I believe that such is the national feeling. This feeling assumes various shapes, but always comes back to that of Union. Once admit the Union, once more acknowledge the authority of the national Government, and, instead of devoting your houses and streets and roads to the dread uses of war, I and this army become at once your protectors and supporters, shielding you from danger, let it come from what quarter it may. I know that a few individuals cannot resist a torrent of error and passion, such as swept the South into rebellion, but you can point out, so that we may know those who desire a government, and those who insist on war and its desolation.

You might as well appeal against the thunder-storm as against these terrible hardships of war. They are inevitable, and the only way the people of Atlanta can hope once more to live in peace and quiet at home, is to stop the war, which can only be done by admitting that it began in error and is perpetuated in pride. . . .

Now you must go, and take with you the old and feeble, feed and nurse them, and build for them, in more quiet places, proper habitations to shield them against the weather until the mad passions of men cool down, and allow the Union and peace once more to settle over your old homes at Atlanta.

GLOSSARY
- **maledictions:** verbal attacks
- **admit:** agree to
- **perpetuated:** continued

★ Philip Sheridan ★

THE LAST BATTLE

From May 1864 until April 1865, Ulysses S. Grant and the Union army gradually wore down Robert E. Lee and his Army of Northern Virginia. By March 1865, Lee was very close to defeat. His army was outnumbered and trapped. Lee knew that if he could march his soldiers to Lynchburg, Virginia, for supplies, he might be able to hold off the Union army. He was intercepted by General Philip Sheridan's cavalry, which was able to hold off the Army of Northern Virginia until Union reinforcements arrived and blocked off all escape routes. Facing impossible odds, Lee surrendered to Grant on April 9, at Appomattox Courthouse. In this excerpt from his official report, Sheridan describes the last day of the Civil War.

- **Philip H. Sheridan, Report on the Appomattox Campaign, in *The War of the Rebellion*, series I, 53 volumes. Washington: Government Printing Office, 1880–1901.**

I rode to the front, near Appomattox Court-House, and just as the enemy in heavy force was attacking the cavalry with the intention of breaking through our lines, I directed the cavalry, which was dismounted, to fall back gradually, resisting the enemy, so as to give time for the infantry to form its lines and march to the attack, and when this was done to move off to the right flank and mount. This was done, and the enemy discontinued his attack as soon as he caught sight of our infantry. I moved briskly around the left of the enemy's line of battle, which was falling back rapidly, heavily pressed by the advance of the infantry, and was about to charge the trains and the confused mass of the enemy, when a white flag was presented to General Custer, who had the advance, and who sent the information to me at once that the enemy desired to surrender.

Riding over to the left at Appomattox Court-House I met Major-General Gordon, of the rebel service. . . [He] requested a suspension of hostilities pending negotiations for a surrender then being held between Lieutenant- General Grant and General Lee. I notified him that I desired to prevent the unnecessary effusion of blood, but as there was nothing definitely settled in the correspondence, and as an attack had been made on my lines with the view to escape, under the impression our force was only cavalry, I must have some assurance of an intended surrender. This General Gordon gave, by saying that there was no doubt of the surrender of General Lee's army. I then separated from him, with an agreement to meet these officers again in half an hour, at Appomattox Court-House. At the specified time, in company with General Ord, who commanded the infantry, I again met this officer, also Lieutenant-General Longstreet, and received from them the same assurance, and hostilities ceased.

GLOSSARY
- **rebel service:** Confederate army
- **pending:** while awaiting
- **effusion:** spilling

FOR FURTHER READING

Books

Bruce Adelson, *George Gordon Meade*. Bloomall, PA: Chelsea House, 2001. A biography focusing on Meade's role as commander of the Army of the Potomac during the final two years of the war.

Dynise Balcavage, *Philip Sheridan*. Bloomall, PA: Chelsea House, 2001. This biography gives particular attention to Sheridan's Shenandoah Valley campaign of 1864, in which Union forces destroyed Confederate supplies in Virginia.

Carl Green and William R. Sanford, *Union Generals of the Civil War*. Berkeley Heights, NJ: Enslow, 1998. Provides short biographies for the best-known Union generals.

Brent Kelley, *George McClellan*. Bloomall, PA: Chelsea House, 2001. In this biography, particular attention is given to McClellan's role as Union military leader during the first year of the war and his role as President Abraham Lincoln's Democratic opponent in the 1864 U.S. presidential campaign.

David C. King, *Ulysses S. Grant*. San Diego, CA: Blackbirch Press/Gale Group, 2002. This biography places emphasis on how Grant's actions affected, and were affected by, other historical personalities and events.

David C. King, *William T. Sherman*. San Diego, CA: Blackbirch Press/Gale Group, 2002. This biography addresses Sherman's long friendships with generals who served on both sides of the Civil War.

Websites

The American Civil War Homepage
http://sunsite.utk.edu/civil-war The largest online directory of Civil War resources, maintained by Dr. George H. Hoemann of the University of Tennessee. Includes biographical information on Union generals.

The Civil War Home Page
http://www.civil-war.net A database of Civil War history, with detailed information on specific battles and campaigns.

INDEX